GUIDE OF THOUGHTS

RAHUL B. R.

Contents

Contents

Contents

Preface

The book "GUIDE OF THOUGHTS" upholds the thoughts and imagination
on love, life, nature and much more. It shows the out of box view in each things
moreover love towards things and journey process.
Shows up the unknown and unseen imaginary thoughts
with well defined explanation.

About Author

Rahul B.R

He is Rahul.B.R He was born on 19/09/1999 Ramanagara district, Karnataka. But he is perceiving his higher studies in Bangalore. He has completed bachelor degree in science. He like to know more about literature and want to study more and more about it... He started writing poems from past four years and he writes all kinds of poems... on life, about nature's beauty, love and much more. He is coauthored in many books, Compiler of the book called "The Song Of Nature", "Nemophilist", "The Song Of Paradise", "Wings To Your Thoughts" and "The Unchosen Bond" and few more... and his poems has been published in his college magazine too.

1. MY LOVE TO YOU

I loved you,
Not because you are rich.
I loved you,
Not because you are poor.
I loved you,
Not because you are beautiful.
I loved you,
Not because you are cute.
I loved you,
Not because you are smart.
I loved you,
Not because you are famous.
I loved you,
Because you deserved to be loved.
I loved you,
Because you are trustworthy.
I love you,
Even if you say no.
I love you,
Even if you say leave.
I love you,
Even if you blame.
I love you,
Even if you don't accept.

I love you,
Even if I die.
I love you
Even if I am far.
I love you,
Even If you doubt.
I love you,
Even if you are no more
-Rahul B R.

2. Happy Holi

Today is Holi,
So let's enjoy fully.
Without making other's suffer,
Let's play with colour .
Many friends get added,
To destroy the black shade,
And to make us fully coloured.
It's the best day and time,
To get good picture and team.
Let's make the world new,
Including the colour blue.
So, I wish Happy Holi to all of you.
-Rahul B R

3. YOUR INNOCENT SMILE

Your smile,
Is my everything.
The way you smile,
Is truly incomparable.
Your innocent smile,
Will make us smile.
May be for a while,
But it's enough for us.
Your smile is filled with meaning,
Including all the thing.
It's one of the immortal smile
And also amazing one.
I have fallen on your smile,
Not just for a while.
It has become my life,
Which keeps me inspiring and safe.
Your innocent smile
Will show what you are made of,
Its not for the show-of...
Your smile says
You too smile,
In all the situation,

Not just now or for a while.

- Rahul B R

4. WHEN IT SNOWS

When it snows,
There is a drastic change.
In the surroundings,
From here to the ending.
All the tree leaf falls,
Due to the coldness.
People blow fire in-front,
To survive and to be warm.
Children play here and there,
And feel happy forever.
They never care for time,
Playing with snow is like a beautiful dine.
Fight with snowball,
Is like common for all.
Making a snowman,
Is like fun for them.
No matter how much cold it is,
Or the snow falls,
Playing in that situation
Is like incomparable one.
Our mind just focuses on play,
And to clear the way,
Snowing is like a dream
But we search it, from where it came...

- Rahul B R

5. SERENDIPITY

I was alone,
With lots of pain.
I din't know what to gain,
And how to gain.
Fame was like unknown,
Because I did know none.
I was disappointed,
At the other end I was not pointed.
But I got inspired by you,
Knowingly or unknowingly by you,
After meeting you.
I din't searched for you,
But met unknowingly.
May be a luck,
Or may be an accident.
But having you is like proud,
Which no-one ever had experienced.
After you came in my life,
I became wise and worthy.
It may be a fluke,
Or may be my good luck,
Or may be a blessing,
To have you in my side.
I have no words,

What to say and what to leave,
And have no clue,
I just surrender in-front of you.
-Rahul B R

6. SMALL THINGS

There are no small things,
Everything has it's own views.
There is nothing worse,
There is nothing best.
Each and everything has value,
Which shows one or the other clue.
So give them equal respect,
And make sure they are perfect.
It's not how much it cost,
Make sure it's the best.
Not the thing which is worst,
Because a small thing can make a big change.
A small success can
Give happiness,
And even a small mistake,
Can make you go downwards.
Make sure when you choose…
It's not the height or weight,
It's the importance
Which comes under picture.
Be always wise to accept,
Whatever comes in front.
Doesn't matter small or big,
See positivity in what you get.

A small earthworm,
Makes the field fertile.
A small virus,
Can kill the so called humans.
A small lie…
Can break any bond.
A bit of small negative word,
Can break the whole trust.
Small looks like negligence,
But, can do unimaginable things.
So always be careful.
- Rahul B R

7. LAUGH

You are the one,
Came like unknown. Made me laugh and well,
When I was ill…
You supported each time,
And came to upload everytime,
You are my true friend,
Our relationship will never end.
Gave me the inspection,
When I was not known.
Gave me support and made me smile,
When I got fail…
Just your presence,
Is enough for my sense.
I get hope with sudden smile,
Even if you come near me for a while.
I need nothing,
When you are with me.
Just a bit see,
You are my only thing.
I don't know how to thank you,
The way you made me laugh,
And the way you inspired,
It's just amazing as I said.
Life without laugh,

Is just like a drought.

So smile a bit,

Even if you don't want it.

-Rahul B R

8. THE LAST TIME

The last time we talked,
Was a bit unusual.
I was a bit nervous,
And couldn't talk straight.
I had many things,
But never said any of those.
Due to inconvenience,
I was a bit out of sense.
But the talk of last time,
Made my day and time.
Happy till now,
And of course forever
That's for sure.
No matter how much close we are,
But, Whenever I come in-front of you,
I feel a bit nervous,
And my words get stuck.
The last time we talked,
Was on the future plans.
The success and goals,
And about our dreams.
The last talk was my best part,
Which can't be erased.
Because it as become the part of life,

And it will be till the end.
Your last talk,
Made me wise enough to think.
To choose the best one,
Not the unknown one.
-Rahul B R

9. HAPPINESS

Happiness is not something,
Which comes everytime.
Being happy is good,
But being too much is bad.
Be a bit wise,
To find happiness,
In every situation.
Happiness is everywhere,
It's inside us.
Uphold it,
And spread it everywhere.
The more happy you are,
More you will be secure.
Happiness is the only medicine,
To make every disease fine.
Think twice or thrice,
It's the happiness,
Which comes,
Now and forever in lives.
-Rahul B R

10. BEGINNING

A new beginning,
Should have something,
Which includes each and everything.
A startup beginning,
Should not be an ending.
It should show,
The capacity and capabilities,
Of you and your willpower.
Neglecting the other,
Now and forever.
It should be with silence,
In both ups and downs.
Should have believe and hopes,
To fulfil the wishes.
Should be wise enough,
To choose the paths,
And should be brave,
To accept all the challenges.
Once it starts,
There should be no words,
Of taking or going back.
Because, we all know
The beginning is not
Just like a piece of cake.

Should be stable,
Humble and acceptable,
In each and everything situation.
Because, no-one knows
What comes on...
-Rahul B R

11. OUR INDIA

Our India,
Our mother land.
The love will never end.
It has gave everything,
Never made us disappointing.
It has vast natural beauty,
Which no-one like to make dirty.
Each and everything is beautiful,
And moreover colourful,
I love my India a lot..
Till my last breath,
Until my death.
It may be a developing country,
But truly shares a lot very,
Each and everything,
Each one of the thing,
Is always amazing.
No one can compare it,
Because it's in the top of it.
Legends are born here,
You can't find no where.
Our India has it's own value,
For which we have no clue.
No matter what we do,

It should be for our, mother land and so.

12. TWINKLING STAR

Twinkle twinkle little star,
I am wandering, where you are.
You always shine in the black sky,
Everytime I see you and feel shy.
You always look like crystal flight,
So I call you, a white shining kite.
Always seen after the burning sun,
Your twinkling light make me warm.
No-matter how far you are,
But I feel you are always near.
You shine each and every night,
With your beautiful twinkling light.
My wish is to have a twinkling star,
So that I can keep it near.
-Rahul B R

13. THE DAWN

Dawn is the true heaven,
And the beautiful one,
The rising sun…
Give relief from pain.
It's an amazing view,
Which can't be guessed with a clue.
No-matter how many times the sun sets,
The dawn will come, that's the fact.
If once we see that site,
Our eyes gets addict to it.
The water drops on the plants,
Makes us feel they are shining pearls.
The dawn makes us feel free,
No-matter how many times we see.
Its truly an awesome creation,
By the mother nature alone.

- *Rahul B R*

14. DECEMBER MONTH

December, the last month...
And also a beautiful month,
All the month stays apart,
When it comes to it.
Me and my friends gather,
And makes the moment memorable forever,
They all bring gifts,
On the day of Christmas nights.
December brings Christmas,
Which is like a pleasure to us.
It's the best and last month to all,
With the weather cold and chill.
It's one of the peaceful month,
And the snow falling month.
True happiness lies here,
Not there or somewhere.
So always be aware,
December is best forever.

- *Rahul B R*

15. MY FIRST PROPOSAL

My first proposal was a bit bad,
Because I was too much scared.
I din't even know what I said,
The situation made me dead.
Sometimes I laugh by remembering that day,
And laugh at my proposed way,
But it was the best experience,
Which made me strong and wise.
I became happy after my proposal,
Because she accepted with being cool.
The happiness came from my pure soul,
Then the days became happier than dull.
After the proposal I was glad,
That with my willpower I did!
As the result it din't failed,
We both are happy now with well balanced.

- *Rahul B R*

16. THE TRAIN JOURNEY

Few days back I travelled in train,
To reach my home town soon.
To be said I am fond of train journeys,
Because it gives me beautiful experiences.
I love to sit near the windows,
To see the amazing views.
We can see mountains, rivers and buildings
And it gives a great feel of blowing winds.
I like train journey the most,
Because it saves the time for the best.
The journey gives joy and relief
And also it's purely safe.
May be in local train it's hard,
About that I can't say a word.
But to be frank the journey will be cool
And it settles the peace inside our hearts.

- *Rahul B R*

17. CANDLE LIGHT DINNER

Once my girl invited me,
I asked where and why.
She said, don't ask questions,
Just come and go once.
I was like what it could be,
Without lots of questions,
I went to see.
The hundreds of candles were lighted,
It was so beautiful to eyesight.
She made me to sit face to face,
And I was left with no clues.
I sat with her with beautiful feeling,
But my hands and legs were shivering,
Because it was my first experience,
And she was looking like an angel ofcourse.
The situation made me express the feelings,
And made the bond more strong between us.
We had a beautiful expressive talk,
Without any scared or shock.
Surrounding made us to feel free,
It was unbelievable to see.
We had a good time together,

And made the day memorable forever.

18. Quotes for Brother

1. BROTHER

A brother is a true friend,
Gifted by the God.
So always care and guide him,
By saying what is good and bad,
By ignoring the count of fight ,
Because we know we love him a lot.

- *Rahul B R*

2.) BROTHER
I don't need anyone,
When I have my brother as my own.
We are two body one soul,
Together we make the life beautiful,
And lead the life with cool.

- *Rahul B R*

3.) BROTHER
I have a younger brother,
Who always make me to face the danger.

And he is a bit lier,
But I love him a lot forever.

- *Rahul B R*

4.) BROTHER

My dear brother..
There are thousands of words to say,
And I always pray,
For you and for your wellbeing,
Because except you I have nothing.

- *Rahul B R*

19. TOGETHER

I will never leave,
Because I am in love.
The love of care,
Which always dare.
Will hold forever,
That's for sure…
You are my love,
As white as dove.
With the believe,
With you always live.

- *Rahul B R*

20. HEALING POWER

Love and happiness,
Are the true healing powers.
They make you wise,
And make you gain happiness.
The love of a mother,
And the care of father,
Has the power,
To heal the pain apart.
These two things,
Can make big changes.
They are incomparable,
And truly unbelievable.
There is no medicine,
When compared to it.
Its long way to go,
To compare it and so.
There is no need,
Of medicine or herb.
When there is love with care,
Now and forever.

- *Rahul B R*

21. ABOUT ME

I am Peacock,
Don't be shock…
One of the beautiful bird,
Also called as Indian national bird.
Body with colourful shade,
To describe me there is no word…
Rich in beauty,
Colour is plenty.
People likes me,
They always love me…

- *Rahul B R*

22. GOD

There is only one God,
Who destroy all shades.
Always be there to uphold peace,
And to fulfil our wish.
We call the all mighty,
By being the devotee...
God has its own beauty,
With the protecting duty.
We can find God in all,
Because God is in everyone's soul.
Always keeps an eye on us ,
To show us the way,
And to wish the bless.
From small things,
To the largest of large things,
Is created by God,
Even including a small piece of wood.
There is both,
Good as well as bad,
It's the believe,
And the mindset,
Of what we all choose.
God never comes in front,
In front of you,

Or in front of me,
But always there to care,
So always be aware.
Never doubt,
The God is there or not,
And never ask what what…
Always remember,
God is in each and every person,
Just need devotion of vision.
No matter how much poor,
Or how much rich you are…
We all are the one,
Other than that there is no one.

- *Rahul B R*

23. A CUP OF COFFEE

It is not just coffee,
It's the medicine to make mind free...
It gives excitement,
In all the event.
It's the best way to refresh,
And to make mind wash.
It taste lovingly,
More over lightly.
Over drinking is addiction,
It comes without saying anyone.
There are loses together,
More than anyone another.
Who grows coffee seeds,
Which always gives such nice yields.
Daily a cup of coffee,
Keeps tension away.
It is scientifically proved,
But not to drink too much hard.
I am a coffee lover too,
Hot and cold too...
Nothing can compete with it,
And nothing is compared to it...

- *Rahul B R*

24. I LOST MYSELF

I lost myself,
In search of you.
Don't know what to do,
I just love you.
Lost myself...
Because of you,
Still safe,
That too because of you.
Lost myself,
By caring you.
No worries,
Because I have you.
I lost myself,
In comforting you.
As per my clue,
I am alive...
That's because of you.
I lost myself,
By seeing you.
Now inside my heart,
It's only you.
Even if I am lost,
And even in the worst.
You will be protected,

In that there is no doubt…

- ***Rahul B R***

25. SISTERS

Sisters are not someone,
They are our own...
Sometimes burn like sun,
And sometimes love with fun.
If they are truly gone,
Then we will be alone.
If they are always on,
Its truly like a boon.
The places will be like heaven,
Sisters are the only one...
Who can shine like moon.
Dear sister...
I breath for you,
And live for you.
You are my everything,
And the goal too...
To make you happy,
I am there for you.
I like your everything,
Not just few things.
Dear little sister,
You made me true warrior.
By being the barrier,
In all the danger...

You are best in culture,
With cuteness in behaviour.
When she is near,
Nothing will bother.
No-one is familiar,
You are my true power.

- ***Rahul B R***

26. COME VISIT ME ONCE

Come visit me once,
Please just once.
I am all yours,
There are no others.
Wish to see you,
And want to be with you.
I don't want to loose you,
With you I want to move.
Visit me once,
Just face to face,
It's my wish.
Just once at least once,
Before I ask twice.
Come visit me,
And please do see...
I won't ask anything,
I don't even need something,
Just I want to spend time,
Like to visit as same.

- *Rahul B R*

27. DIGITAL MONEY

In this modern world,
Everything is like bold.
Smart and improved,
By thinking it broad.
Everything is digitalized,
Everything has craze.
Everything has value,
Nothing is low...
Digital money,
Is with many.
Online pay, online booking...
No cash and carrying.
Within blink of a second,
Will be finished.
Now no to post,
Digital money is best.
Safe and secure,
With lots of improve.
Best and safe,
With OTP codes.

- *Rahul B R*

28. MY LIFE IS A POEM

My life is a poem,
With love and fame.
Not like the same,
It's filled with calm.
With lots of imagination,
With lots of fun.
With lots of experience,
With hard defence.
Not the meaningless,
Not even a case.
Filled with cares,
With loving essence…
Hard to understand,
Runs with no end.
Inspiring the other,
Saying it's not too far.
Describe the things,
With the way of words.
Hard to answer it…
Also to predict.

- *Rahul B R*

29. MASK

In today's world,
It is truly common,
For some or the other one
It's like fun...
Some wear smile,
Some for a while.
Some in dull,
Some with fail.
Mask of sympathy,
Mask of friendliness.
Is purely seen,
Because it's in...
When people are angry,
Or sad with worry,
They hide it from others
By wearing smile masks.
So at least you be yourself,
By motivating yourself...

- *Rahul B R*

30. THE LIFE...

Life is the journey,
With plenty of obstacles.
With good or bad,
With happiness and sad.
It's just not simple,
It's hard but not too hard,
Life is filled with all,
Inclusive light and dull...
Depends on which way you are,
Peace or war.
But always do dare,
To love and to share with care.
Some say worst,
Some say best.
Some only dreamed,
Some do experienced.
Go with time,
It's not always the same.
Hard to believe,
But we should live...

- *Rahul B R*

31. HOMECOMING

I am coming back,
But not for any sake.
It's hard to be far,
More and more...
It is dangerous,
And the worst case.
Living far from home,
So coming home.
Went far to achieve something,
Did a lot in timing.
Saw many a thing,
So now I am Homecoming...
It's bit long time,
No worries, can't blame.
Now it's time to rest,
As fast as fast...
The time has come,
Like as usual the same.
To go back home,
Like the same.

- *Rahul B R*

32. IF I WERE A BUTTERFLY

If I were a butterfly,
I would have fly.
To the beautiful blue sky,
As possible as high…
With the colourful nature,
Going far and far.
Roaming and seeing,
The beauty of nature shining.
Would have sat on flower,
For honey or nectar.
Jumped from flower to flower,
Like an immense lover.
With the little life span,
I would have won.
All the hearts of people,
For sure without fail.
Would have made them smile,
At least for a while.
With my wonderful skill,
Would have made them cool.

- *Rahul B R*

33. PAPER BOAT

It reminds of our childhood,
When we used to play with mud.
Paper boat is also one such thing,
Where we played while raining.
For happiness there was no limit,
Till the ending by following it.
Making paper boat was common,
To have a happy fun.
Those rainy days were the best,
Enjoyment was more than that.
Then making a paper boat,
Was completely an art.
Leaving the boat flow,
As we see it moves slow.
Being wet till the end,
With the boat as well as friend.
For now it has become memories,
Because now no child play this,
It was filled with beautiful experience,
Where no-one can get it twice.
Sometimes filled with danger,
Which never we bother.
Wish to play again for sure,
But there is no water flow here.

34. Quotes on college life

1. ***College days are those days,***

Where no-one cares.
It's the time to do wonders.
So as to has experience.

- ***Rahul B R***

2. ***College life not only teach us how to enjoy,***

But also teach us
How to shape the future.

- ***Rahul B R***

3. ***College life will not teach you everything,***

But of-course it will teach you many things.

- ***Rahul B R***

4. ***People say college life is best,***

But I say it's the best of the best,
Because it's the time to live our lives to the fullest.

- ***Rahul B R***

35. MOON OF EID

It will be beautiful,
With white shine full.
Way of looking,
Can't be explained by anything.
It shines like bright white,
As it's the white shining kite.
Near to it the star,
Uphold the beauty more.
More different from the other days,
By seeing it happiness overflows.
It's highly incomparable,
Beautifully unbelievable.
Shape of it is highlighted,
And also attracted.
Whole sky looks clean,
With all time twinkling shine.

• *Rahul B R*

36. WHEN I WILL MEET GOD

I will ask him…
Not only for mine,
To all of us the same.
To give happiness and fame,
To show love and care,
To bless us with no danger,
To make us succeed,
In all the ongoing and upcoming field.
I will also say him…
I don't need anything,
Just a bit of happiness, and other thing.

- *Rahul B R*

37. ANKLETS

The beautiful silver ring,
With simple structuring.
Part of the tradition,
Which is always known.
Well designed one,
About it what to be known.
Shines with sparking light,
With amazing beautiful white.
Well known to all...
But not completely and full.
After many years it becomes dull,
To us it's like a white pearl.
Some may wear some may not,
Some may ask what's that...
And some may doubt,
But it's always a gift,
So accept it without making hurt.

- *Rahul B R*

38. SUICIDE

We are not coward,
Should have courage to face in board.
What we did,
What should be done
Is all secondary...
Trying to do with level best,
Is always first and primary duty.
Suicide is not solution,
And not end of all in one,
It is not sacrifice too...
It's the cowardly thought of you.
Be honest and brave,
Even when you are slave.
Never encourage your weakness,
Always believe in goodness.

- *Rahul B R*

39. FEATHER

Beauty of feather,
Is not seen all over.
It upholds the beauty of birds,
From small till dragons.
Beautiful feathers,
Has it's own significance.
It attracts all…
From top till the whole full.
Some are killed for feather,
Some are pet for their behaviour.
Some are very danger,
So think before you dare.
Feathers are the part,
For the bird to support.
So don't harm it,
Be happy by looking it.

- *Rahul B R*

40. ONE SIDE CONVERSATION

Always thinking about you,
Like who are you,
What are you,
Where are you.
Asking myself,
To become yours.
Always praying and talking to myself,
And wishing for protection and of being safe.
Always thinking of you,
Don't know what to do,
Talking to myself had become common,
It's like all time one side conversation.
Dreaming and imagining,
Everyday and at every timing.
Hoping for the best situation,
To myself in my one side conversation.

- *Rahul B R*

41. THOSE WERE THE DAYS

Those were the days,
Where there were full of happiness.
Only filled with wishes,
And period of schools.
Playing in ground,
With lots of sound.
No care to anyone,
Should dare to everyone,
Thinking we are the only one.
It was a busy lifestyle,
Without lots of schedule file.
Sleeping in the last row,
Making the others bow.
No limits of the happiness,
No one cares about the size.
Punishment was common,
From one or the other one.
Those days were the best,
Memories are hard to digest.

- *Rahul B R*

42. SOUND OF HEARTBEAT

Sound of heartbeat,
Is just like a target shoot.
It's like a friend to us,
Which stays with us.
When it stops,
There are no wishes.
It's just like lost,
At the end of last.
It's highly sensitive,
And lovely attractive.
Better to safeguard it,
For the betterment of it.
It sounds so calm,
With comfort and warm. Out heartbeat is the best,
So hear till the last.
No one knows when it stops,
No one knows when it breaks,
It's all like an ongoing process,
So to stop it no one dares.
Heartbeat has it's own way,
It's impossible to say.
So just listen and enjoy,

Until we people die.

- ***Rahul B R***

43. MIRROR

Mirror it's not just a glass,
It's the true face...
Which shows what we are,
And how we are...
It's reflects the true character,
Without changing anything or the other.
It never lies to us,
It shows the way it is.
It never creates new,
Or hides the true,
It's the only thing which says truth,
And the true worth.
Many people compare it,
In many different ways.
It's true and it deserves,
Because it's highly focus.
It makes us to thinks deep,
Now and forever.
With its true nature,
It sketches our future.

• *Rahul B R*

44. IF I WAS INVISIBLE

If I was invisible,
I would have done more than able.
Something is not capable,
But using invisibility it's able.
I would have done,
More that I can,
It's not easy and same,
And it's not the matter of fame.
Invisibility is like immortal,
Where no one is capable.
It's like out of thought,
To be like that everyone gets pride.
It's looks simple to think,
Like a invisible blink.
Some may get shrink,
And some may get perfect link.
Invisibility is an amazing thing,
Where all wants to be the same being.
May be it's impossible,
But not highly incapable.

- *Rahul B R*

45. Quotes On INNER BEAUTY

1. ***Inner beauty...***

Is the true beauty,
Which emerges from the character,
And spread all over,
Without any fear.

- ***Rahul B R***

2. ***Nature is the true example..***

For outer and for the inner beauty,
Because it's beauty is incomparable,
And truly unbelievable.

- ***Rahul B R***

3. ***In this present world,***

Inner beauty has no meaning.
As it represents inner,

It has been buried deeper,
So I have no words to say further.

- ***Rahul B R***

4. ***Yes I am not beautiful like you,***

Yes I am not charming like you,
Yes I am not glowing as you,
But my inner beauty is one step ahead than you.

- ***Rahul B R***

46. FLOWERS

Dear flowers,
Bloom fast,
You are the best.
You are incomparable,
Beautifully unbelievable.
The way you are,
It's truly dare.
We are nothing,
In front of you.
You always make us smile,
You are like a happy file.
You live for few days,
But that days are the best once.
You create wonders,
With your fragrance and growths.
Making you to grow,
Is not like a child's play.
It's truly an art,
Where you have to paint.
You are one of the best,
God's and of Nature's creations,
You make us calm,
And keeps us happy and warm.
Your beauty can't be described,

Only the way you are can be described.
Nothing standards besides you,
Because it's you and only you…

- ***Rahul B R***

47. THEATRE ARTISTS

They are the artist,
But not the happiest.
They suffer a lot,
From all kinds of beat.
They try to survive,
With hope and willpower.
But they have enough power;
To become life saviour.
They work-hard day and night,
Without powers and light.
Their life is very hard to lead,
Because it's the war field.

- *Rahul B R*

48. TWO LOVE BIRDS

Two love birds,
Never say many words.
They like silence,
Avoiding the violence.
They see one another,
As they are made for each other.
They can't be separated,
And can't be avoided.
They make their own way,
Within few seconds or a day.
No one can understand them,
They are like light flame.
Contributes many things,
Without saying any words.
Live life as if they are…
Only made for each other.
Two love birds
Never ever depends,
They like the way they are,
And they just move further…

49. CUDDLE LOVE

Never doubt the love,
Have the believe...
It's truly hard to get it,
So never neglect it.
Love can be found,
But true love it's hard.
If you get it by any chance,
Never miss that chance.
Never let it go as your true love,
Hold it within you.
If you loose the true love,
There will be nothing to you.
Until the last breath,
Hold it with worth.
Because some ask for it,
And some tries to take it.
Hold it with simplicity,
And with soft capability,
If it breaks down,
Nothing can be done.

- *Rahul B R*

50. LIVE IN RELATIONSHIP

Sometimes the relationship,
Never goes too deep.
It's hard to carry on
And reach to the maximum.
Yes… sometime,
Relationship may lead to good time.
Who knows what happens,
No one knows what comes and goes.
Relationship always depends,
On the care and understanding bonds.
If something becomes less,
It makes you pay huge price.
Relationship is good,
But not truly bad…
Should have clarity,
Rather than thoughts of being dirty.
It may lead to unknown ends,
Where we can't even imagine those.
Sometimes gives us the hope,
Even when there is no clue of map.

- *Rahul B R*

51. SECRETIVE AFFAIR OF LOVE

It's dangerous,
With lots of obstacles.
With lots of pain,
Where there is nothing to gain.
Some way or the other way,
It comes to an end.
Then there will be nothing to say,
Just we bow bend.
Feels good,
But not truly good.
We can't even say it's bad,
Because it may reach the destiny one day.
Secretive affairs,
May lead to no ways.
Be careful and sharp,
Before taking the forward step.

- *Rahul B R*

52. Quotes On EXPLORING MIND

The exploring mind,
Has no limits.
And it has no restrictions,
To one which is bonded.
- Rahul B R
Exploring brain always thinks new,
And search for some clue.
To make sure to go forward,
To a longer and bigger field.
Rahul B R
The person who has
An exploring mind,
Can survive in all difficulties,
Without any doubt...
-Rahul
Our exploring mind,
Should always have patience.
To think and to decide,
What to do and what not to.
Rahul B R
Exploring mind is not only
Directly proportional to books,

But also proportional to explore/journey.

- Rahul B R

53. TWO WHEELS OF LOVE

Love never withstand,
From just one end.
It needs both the end,
Otherwise it will bend.
Love becomes balanced,
Only when both tries to understand.
They act as two wheels of love,
To carry it forward and move.
If love is from one person,
It has no use and it will be gone.
It loses its capabilities,
If it is not from both sides.
Making it withstand and balanced...
It is very hard.
Because, it needs equal care,
And other things more.

- *Rahul B R*

54. LOVE IS IN AIR

Dear, love is immoral
And pure loyal,
So it is everywhere,
As if it's in air.
Love is present everywhere,
Because it's here, there and everywhere.
Love can't be seen,
But we can feel it.
In the same way,
The air too…
Love is in air,
Just feel it brother.
Don't search here and there,
Just be loyal and show care.

- *Rahul B R*

55. LOVE, THE TRUE LOVE

Love is blind,
Sometimes may not be kind.
True love hard to find,
So never lose your strong bond.
True love will never end
And will never make you bend,
Sometimes it asks everything…
May be by knowing or unknowing.

- *Rahul B R*

56. BABY

They are true pure soul,
Such a calm and cool.
They don't know anything,
Except just seeing.
Like them there is none,
Till now and then.

- *Rahul B R*

57. SOUL

It's us,
Not someone or the others…
It's the true identity,
Of our own self.
It's the inner one,
Sometimes it's known to be none…

- ***Rahul B R***

Printed by Libri Plureos GmbH in Hamburg,
Germany